Like bullies sent to the principal's office for fighting, these three Pz.Kpfw.IV's deposited in a field *"two miles south of Trévières"* are chastised but unrepentant. The Panzer on the left first appeared on page 17 of *Panzerwrecks 1* and belonged to 6.SS-Pz.Rgt.2. It was knocked out during an encounter with the US 117th Infantry Regiment of the 30th Infantry Division on the outskirts of Saint-Fromond in July 1944. At the time, the 30th was supported the 743rd Tank Battalion and the 823rd Tank Destroyer Battalion (M10). The middle tan the same as the one on page 1. This feature, from pages 2 to 29, is based on Signal Co motion picture film shot in July 1944.

NA

en from twenty yards away, the damage on the left Pz.Kpfw.IV '6X5' is apparent, rticularly to the cupola, mantlet and superstructure front. The turret 'Schürzen' has o been peeled back. Overall though, the vehicles brought to this collection point appear etty much intact. As will be seen in the photos on pages 10-11, the middle vehicle is an

Ausf.H with tactical number '631' on the turret 'Schürzen' and the division's 'Wolfsangel' emblem on the left rear corner of the engine compartment. The third vehicle is an Ausf.J with tactical number '622' as seen on pages 12-13. A 'Selbstfahrlafette für 2cm Flak 38' appears on the left, complete with Allied star.

NARA

Opposite page: As '6X5' fills the frame we learn more about it: the 'Fahrgestell' number the driver's visor, '89689,' identifies it as an Ausf.J. Besides the hole in the front superstructure, others appear below the mantlet and on the turret side. The barrel sleeve, broken free of the recuperator housing and swathed in chicken wire, is almost to the muzzle brake, allowing us to see the unpainted portion of the barrel normally hidden by the sleeve. **This page:** A tow cable runs across the superstructure front and hangs down along the side of '631.' On the right is a Ford 3000S 'Maultier.'

2x NARA

5

A view of the third Pz.Kpfw.IV, tact number '622.' The mangled railing for its superstructure mounted 'Schürzen' will help to identify it in other views. This vehicle is more or less complete with little sign of damage. Dropping the 'Filzbalgfilter' with the Ausf.H allowed spare road wheels to be carried on the right side. The open doors in the turret mounted 'Schürzen' give the turret a much wider appearance. Bits of branches and foliage can seen on the turret roof. Note that the hatches on the cupolas on all of these vehicles a almost upright in their positions. **Opposite page:** A close-up view of '6X5.' The lines in t 'Zimmerit' are smooth and virtually unbroken, like ripples in desert sand dunes. **2x NA**

88

posite page: The details speak volumes. The 'Fahrgestell' number on '6X5' is repeated the track support bracket, and a hatch door rests under the hull MG. Tangled chicken re obscures the tactical number on the turret 'Schürzen.' **This page:** Rear view of the rd Pz.Kpfw.IV showing the truncated cap welded over the hole for the auxiliary muffler that was dropped on Ausf.J production. Chicken wire covers the turret 'Schürzen' and part of a tactical number can been seen beneath the foliage. The head-pad has dropped away from the cupola hatch. **Pages10-11:** Two detail views of '631', note the 2.SS-Panzer-Division 'Wolfsangel' marking on the rear plate. **2x NARA**

Pages 12-13: Pz.Kpfw.IV '622' is parked next to an armoured 'schwerer Geländegängiger Lastkraftwagen 4·5 t für Flak (Sf)' mounting a 3·7cm Flak 36. **This page:** The cameraman steps back to record the white sheet hanging from the radio antenna. Chicken wire retains foliage on the turret but other branches are simply stuck in the idler adjusting assemb Note the turret doors still retain their vision devices at this stage of the war and m packs the tracks.

3x NA

e divisional insignia is again seen on the rear of '622.' From this angle we can see the nt portion of the 'Schürzen' on '631' and the hole in the turret of '6X5'. **Pages 16-**

17: Detail view of running gear: '6X5's on page 16 and '631's on page 17. These can be differentiated because '6X5's track has been fitted backwards. **3x NARA**

...de views of a 4·7cm Pak(t) auf Panzerkampfwagen 35R(f) ohne Turm showing the ...mmo stowage in a compartment built out over the engine deck. At least one side door ...missing, though the hinges remain. Note the armoured door over the gun sight is in the ...sed position and that the gun itself is completely out of battery. **Page 20:** Close up of

the hand-painted vehicle specs and alternate nomenclature, 'Kfz.Sfl.(35R).' The only unit reporting these vehicles in Normandy was 3./Schnelle Abt.517 (Schnelle Brig. 30).

3x NARA

age 21: Rear view of a Panzerjäger 38(t) mit 7·5cm Pak 40/3 Ausf.M (Sd.Kfz.138) with ctical number '111.' Note the symbol of full tracked anti-tank unit on the lower left d the white painted corners. **Opposite page:** Front view showing battle damage. The und, cast cover for the driver's compartment means this vehicle was produced in 1943.

Note the tactical symbol repeated on the edge of the lower superstructure. **Inset:** A view through the shattered front plate. **This page:** A more general view of the vehicle showing again the large patches of dark camouflage in the three tone paint scheme. It belonged to 1st Kompanie of either Pz.Jg.Abt.243, 326, 346, 352 or 353 (Inf.Divs.) **4x NARA**

This StuG.III Ausf.G is the second of two such vehicles that we showed on page 26 of *Panzerwrecks 1*, the identifier being the shape of the front mudguards. In *PW1* we gave the location as Cerisy-la-Forêt. Based on Fred Deprun's research, this scrapyard was probably near a railway like others in Normandy, in the vicinity of the big marshalling yar at Le Molay-Littry. The waffle patterned 'Zimmerit' was applied only by the firm of Alket Possible unit ID: Stu.Gesch.Abt.1352 or Fallsch.Stu.Gesch.Brig.12.

2x NAR

This is the first vehicle shown on page 26 of *Panzerwrecks 1*. Part of the fighting compartment roof is propped up in the engine compartment, affording us a clear view of the loader's MG shield and the two positions for his MG. Note the paint scheme continued onto the roof. This StuG has the unribbed, perforated steel return rollers introduced by Alkett in January, 1944. **Opposite:** A study in textures. StuG '8' belonged to Fallsch.Stu Gesch.Brig.12, which fought between Saint-Lô and Chaumont-L'éventé. **2x NAR**

wo views of a Selbstfahrlafette (Sd.Kfz.10/4) für 2cm Flak 38 with wider gun platform and acket mounted turn signals. Note how the corner fillet of the drop side gun platform folded against the side panel. The cover for the fender mounted rifle rack is missing. The 2cm Flak 38 could be removed if the vehicle was to serve as a load carrier. **2x NARA**

'LSSAH' operated this mittlerer Schützenpanzerwagen (Sd.Kfz.251) which was apparently abandoned in good condition, other than a shredded fender, in the Polish sector, along with a leichter Schützenpanzerwagen (Sd.Kfz.250) and another m.S.P.W. The le.S.P.W., pla number WH-1728224, tactical number 'XX2' or 'X2,' is believed to be from Pz.A.A.2. **PIS**

GI's can only imagine what happened to this mittlerer Schützenpanzerwagen (7·5cm Kanone) (Sd.Kfz.251/9) Ausf.D that has come apart like a wet cardboard box somewhere between Villebaudon and Percy on 4 August. The entire left side, where the 7·5cm ammo box was secured, and the floor plates housing the torsion bars, have been ripped away to reveal the gun mount and twisted fuel can in the interior.   **NARA**

The Pz.Kpfw.IV was the predominant German AFV in the Normandy area and suffered commensurate losses trying to stem the Allied advance. This photo gives a good idea of the terrain and combat distances involved in the fighting. Pz.Kpfw.IV Ausf.J, tactical number '735,' from 7./SS-Pz.Rgt.2 was knocked out between St-Denis-le-Gast and Gavray, and pushed off the road some time before this photo was taken. The rear turret 'Schürze has been blown to an unusual angle by an explosion in the engine compartment. One the return rollers is missing. 'Zimmerit' applied to the lower hull but not to the upper si of the engine compartment or turret sides indicates an early Ausf.J. **L.Archer/W.Auerba**

Tank '741,' a Pz.Kpfw.IV Ausf.J from 7./SS-Pz.Rgt.1 of 1.SS-Panzer-Division, was most likely Ustuf. Werner Kothmann's tank, as he was leader of the 4th platoon during Normandy. It was left in a field between Chambois and Saint-Lambert-sur-Dives, and serves now as an observation platform for Canadian soldiers. An Allied shell has penetrated the superstructure next to the radio operator's position, probably setting the tank alight, which goes some way to explaining the black scorch marks around the hatches and mantlet. These scorch marks contrast against the light colour of the tank. The meaning of the number '131' on the side of the engine compartment is unknown.

2x L.Archer/W.Auerbach

A GI inspects a knocked out Pz.Kpfw.IV, possibly an Ausf.H, with the remains of a broken tow bar still attached. Graffiti on the turret 'Schürzen' appears to read: *"974 on 7/31/44. St.Lo."* Although other US units in France had the 974th designation, we believe the graffiti refers to the 974th Ordnance Evacuation Company which operated under the US VII Corps in the Normandy sector collecting wrecks. In fact, Ernie Pyle, the famous w correspondent, may have witnessed the recovery of this same wreck. Note spare tra links covering the driver's front plate and turret front, the same as the Pz.Kpfw.IV's c pages 73 - 76 of *Panzerwrecks 8*.

D.Brow

he same scene as the previous page, except part of the wall in the background has sappeared. The spare road wheels and towing clevises are also missing. Using filters, a nt tactical number '11' was teased out of the background murk, leading us to believe is Pz.Kpfw.IV is one from Pz.Lehr's I.Stabsregiment or Stabsabteilung II./Pz.Rgt.130.

Note the unusual placement of the 'Balkenkreuz' behind the spare road wheel rack and the open door on the engine compartment. Many Pz.Kpfw.IV's lost their side skirts in the bocage, and Allied reports mentioned that the more resourceful infantrymen were using them as covers for their foxholes.
L.Archer/W.Auerbach

A GI poses for the camera against a Sturmgeschütz IV from SS-Pz.Abt.17, 17.SS-Panzergrenadier-Division. The only markings are a 'Balkenkreuz' on the side of the superstructure and a rhomboid marking on the left trackguard indicating the 1.Kompan The vehicle is missing the left track, but other than that appears to be in good shape. **AN**

According to Schneider's *Tiger im Kampf - Normandie*, these photos show Tiger '111' of s.H.Pz.Abt.503 that was abandoned in an orchard near Le Billot on 18 August and photographed by a Canadian officer. Note the war wounds on the hull front: one can only imagine how the Allied gunner felt seeing his shells bounce off. **3x LAC**

Tiger II, tactical number '122,' of s.H.Pz.Abt.503 and M4A4 Sherman 'Ballyragget' of 2nd Battlalion, Irish Guards, near Emiéville, east of Cagny. There is some debate about the incident on 18 July, but the Tiger either backed into the M4, or the M4 rammed the Tiger. Suffice to say that the two came to blows, and the Tiger was subsequently brewed either by a German Pak or a 'Firefly'. **4x LAC**

The Tiger II, wIth the turret designed for the Porsche Tiger, burned out, as evidenced by the flaked 'Zimmerit' and scorched appearance. Note the light, horizontal band two thirds the way down the turret. Canadian Intell remarked on the *"steel tired bogie wheels incorporating rubber in sheer,"* and noted that, *"A total of 5 Tiger II tks have been seen on the Cdn Army front by the AFV(T) Staff to date. One of these was found near Cagny just southeast of Caen and the others in the Falaise area. All were burnt out and no internal detail was obtainable."* **LAC**

A very sorry looking Tiger lies on the Quai Jean de Béthencourt at Rouen docks. The docks were the subject of heavy bombing by the RAF on or around 25 August, leading to the devastation of the German units trying to cross the Seine. A drive sprocket and length of track have parted company, and, somewhat unusually, the nose armour has been blow away giving a unique glimpse of the steering gear. This Tiger reportedly carried tactic number '341' and was used by Ustuf. Schienhofen of 3./s.SS-Pz.Abt.102. **F.Malivo**

nother dead Tiger at Rouen docks courtesy of the RAF. This one has been identified as elonging to 3./s.SS-Pz.Abt.102 (the outline of a number '3' can be seen on the turret side and the font matches the unit style). Nearly all of the 'Zimmerit' coating has come off of the nose and driver's front plate. Just a small patch remains by the headlamp. **F.Malivoir**

...ger '114' of 1./s.SS-Pz.Abt.101 was captured by the British after ...ing damaged outside Fontenay-le-Pesnel on 26 June. The tank ...s then shipped to the UK for trials, where these photos were ...ken. Interesting details of note are the damage to the road wheels, scruffy condition of the paintwork, unit and tactical insignia on the rear plate, and what remains of the tactical number underneath the stencilled area on the turret side. The unique trailer distributed the load evenly side to side and front to back. **6x LAC**

FOR OB
TRIAL
NO AP (A)
189

A Bergepanther found abandoned outside the local dairy/grocery store. Its 'Zimmerit' was applied with a diagonal cross grid, and British or Canadian troops have daubed graffiti where large patches wore off the glacis plate. Between the driver's visor and radio operator's MG flap are the six bolts for mounting a 2cm Kw.K. Note the small tie-downs at the top of the glacis plate, and how there are no AA MG mounts atop the perisco[pe] covers. This vehicle lacks the wooden drop-side superstructure normally mounted ov[er] the winch compartment, which allows us to see the pair of Panther road wheels stow[ed] there.

2x TT

44

The trident of the 2.Panzer-Division appears when the coil of rope is moved. The photo on the opposite page was taken by a Canadian technical intelligence team after the vehicle was relocated, probably not far away. Note the warnings chalked on the hull 'Schürzen.'

1x TTM, 1x LAC

On the previous pages, we saw the warnings, *"Boob
Trap," "Keep Off,"* and *"Danger HE,"* chalked on th
side of this Bergepanther being ignored by a Canadia
soldier. Here he is more cautious as he inspects th
massive unditching beam carried on the right side
the vehicle. (Other Bergepanthers carried the bea
on the left side and the dismantled jib boom cra
on the right.) The bracket above the lock and cha
held a long handled sledge-hammer. There are
brackets to hold 'Schürzen' to protect this side of t
hull, and the area between the top of the track a
the bottom of the sponson is an inviting target.

L

ose up view of the 'Schürzen' on the left
de showing how it was locked in place with a
ock of steel bolted to the inner bracket. The
mmerit' pattern is quite apparent here, as is
at 2.Panzer-Division trident.

LAC

The business end of a Bergepanther. It has th[e]
bracket for the cable guide rollers between th[e]
mufflers and the sturdy brackets on each si[de]
of the lower hull for the pivoting spade, but n[o]
spade per se. The mangled bit of metal over th[e]
left track was the cylindrical rear convoy lig[ht.]
Note the hook and chain attached to the cab[le]
guide bracket and the jerry-can on the engi[ne]
deck behind it.

L[A]

The guts of the winch compartment on a different Bergepanther, captured near Vimoutiers with a Tiger II. This one has the drop side wooden enclosure around the platform covering the winch. **Top:** Looking towards the right side of the vehicle. **Bottom:** Looking towards the rear of the vehicle. **2x LAC**

Standing on the engine deck and looking into the winch compartment. The cable take-up drum is on the left and the cable ran out through the hole on the right. The pulleys could be used to double the draw of the 40 ton capacity winch by placing one on the Bergepanther's centre tow coupling and one on the vehicle to be recovered, thus doubling the distance the cable would travel. The front and rear wood sections were staked on rather than hinged to fold down. **LAC**

Autopsy Allied style. A Marder 38T gives up some unique details now it has been almost surgically blown apart. Considering that all but the rear of the fighting compartment has been blown away, the remainder of the vehicle is in good order. The three colour camouflage pattern is easy to see, and the 'Balkenkreuz' on the rear plate is exceptiona[l] clear. These Panzerjäegers were found in Infantry Division, the candidates are: 1./Pz. Abt.243, 326, 346, 352 and 353.

W.Auerba[ch]

other Marder 38T, with squared off welded cover for the driver's compartment, sits
a ditch, its gun firmly cradled in the travel lock. This is a late 1943 or 1944 production
hicle that also had the hull sides extended to form towing eyes. Having about the same armour thickness and distribution as a light or medium armoured personnel carrier, these Panzerjägers would fly apart at the seams if struck by even a light calibre projectile.

L.Archer/W.Auerbach

Two different Panzerkampfwagen 38 für 2cm Flak 38 (Sd.Kfz.140). The one pictured directly above and below is in a sunken lane and does not have its 2cm Flak 38 installed. It was destroyed near La Ferté-Macé. The armour plate with four hinges across the top is part of the (now opened) two piece access hatch over the engine compartment. **2x NARA**

Above: Another Flakpanzer found intact inside the Argentan - Falaise gap. Both have t[...] cast armour cover over the driver's position. Compare it to the cover on the Panzerjäg[...] on page 53. The rectangular brackets are 'interrupters' used to prevent the gun fr[...] depressing beyond a certain point. **2x NA[...]**

The fighting compartment of the same Flakpanzer showing a close up of the 2cm Flak 38 though the weapon itself has been removed. Elevation was -10 to +90 degrees. Instead the gunner's head shield being a flat plate, the one shown here is a 'stepped' affair. The gun has been traversed to the 3 o'clock position, which means we are looking out the back of the vehicle.

NARA

A GI (paratrooper?) reaches inside an abandoned 'Marder I' for an item of interest, a dangerous habit to get into when booby-traps abound. In his left hand he holds a camera he may have just liberated. The location is the locale around Sainte-Mère-l'Église, the unit: 1./Pz.Jg.Abt.709 of the 709.Infanterie-Division, the only unit so equipped in the area. This fully stowed Panzerjäger LrS für 7·5cm Pak 40/1 seems to have been attempting to find concealed position for ambush when it reversed its way into a ditch. Note the ammo an radio gear on the right hand side and the unusual, high contrast pattern camouflage. T broad external gun shield was a distinguishing feature of this Panzerjäger. **USAH**

These three photos, taken by a British soldier, provide a study in camouflage paint schemes. **Top left:** a 'Wespe', tactical number '214' sporting the Trident insignia of 2.Panzer-Division. **Top right:** a Pz.Beob.Wg.III with its turret traversed to the rear. Some camouflage paintwork can be seen on the false gun barrel and large dark splotches are over the rest of the vehicle.

Bottom: a trackless 'Grille' with vertical sheets and splinters of dark colours and the gun letter 'B' indicating it was the 2nd gun in the battery. (Batteries might be colour coded, but were never lettered!) The white circle was painted on by Allied recovery crews and is typical of wrecks found at the Saint-Lambert-sur-Dives dump. **3x D.Trowbridge**

A trio of schwerer Zugkraftwagen (18t) (Sd.Kfz.9) with artistic paint schemes. These prime movers were the mainstay of many recovery outfits, and the loss of any single vehicle would have been a severe blow to their operational capabilities. They were always in constant, heavy use and just as prone to breakdown as any other vehicle, so losing three would have been catastrophic. No cranes or spades appear to have been fitted to any these vehicles, but their raison d'etre was their raw tractive power. Fred Deprun estimat that these vehicles are at a dump in Le Chêne Guérin near Percy, where the Werkstatt Panzer-Lehr was located between 27 and 30 July.

L.Archer/W.Auerba

"US infantryman, rifle ready as he comes warily down the road leading to Avranches, passes a deserted and smoking German halftrack ko'd during the drive to the Brest peninsula." The emblem of the 17.SS-Pz.Gren.Div. appears on the fender of this s.Zgkw. 18t) (Sd.Kfz.9) next to the tactical sign for a Pz.Bergetrupp. The end of a tow bar protrudes from the rear crew seating area. **NARA**

A burnt out Pz.Kpfw.II discovered by the Canadians at Carpiquet airfield in July 1944. Martin Block takes up the story: *"Not long ago I was fortunate to acquire the war diary of SS-Pz.Rgt.12 during the Normandy campaign, and according to an entry on 8.5.1944 the 7 Pz. II that had been in use with the regimental recce platoon so far were distributed as follows: 1 to the regimental Pz.Fla-Zug; 2 to the Werkstatt-Zug; 2 to the I./SS-Pz.Rgt. 12;* *2 to the II./SS-Pz.Rgt. 12. These 7 Pz. II had been on strength since at least Oct 1943. The are barely mentioned again after May 1944 but it is quite possible some survived until Ju For unknown reasons they do not appear in the regular monthly status reports, only in th regimental war diary."*

2x LA

ese two photos were taken by Major W.H. Sale, MC of 3rd/4th County of London omanry (Sharpshooters). Major Sale gives the location as Villons-les-Buissons, but, rough the work of Fred Deprun, we now know that it was just Southwest at Cambes-en- aine. Several Allied soldiers can be seen roaming the grounds and climbing on vehicles, which seem to go on as far as the eye can see. Panthers (with typical 3./SS-Pz.Rgt.12 hooks on the turrets) and Pz.Kpfw.IV's (8./Pz.Rgt.22; see turret door on page 62) are predominant. A section from the superstructure side of the Pz.Kpfw.IV has been removed. A 'Stuart III' is in the foreground opposite and an M10 17 pdr is above on the left. **2x NAM**

This leichter Panzerspähwagen (Fu) (Sd.Kfz.223) Ausf.B, caught by a US motion picture cameraman, first appeared on page 75 of *Panzerwrecks 1,* where we identified the unit as being the SS-Pz.Aufkl.Abt.17 of 17.SS-Panzergrenadier-Division and the location as Isigny - now thought to be on a road near Le Molay-Littry. The supports for the metal frame antenna were made of wood, and an intense fire such as this vehicle suffered wou have made short work of them. Just about every door, hatch and lid has been opened f inspection but for the most part the cupboards are bare. Note the MG mount in the sm one man turret and the 'Balkenkreuz' on the rear armour.

NAR

near mint Selbstfahrlafette (Sd.Kfz.10/5) für 2cm Flak 38 with Luftwaffe licence plate ccupies a corner of the same collection yard. The covers of several 2cm ammo magazines ong the sidewall of the gun platform, as well as the cover on the fender mounted rifle rack and even the lid of a valise, have been popped open by the curious who seem to have walked off with the cushion for the driver's seat. The narrow front wheels always give these vehicles a spindly look.

NARA

All manner and type of armoured and softskinned vehicles made their way into these dumps, some more gently than others. Here are two Marder 38Ts that once formed the backbone of the Panzerjäger units in Normandy. No markings of any kind are visible.

NA

hile most vehicles, artillery pieces and individuals hew to the treeline for shade, two GI's nture out into the sun to check under the hood of a Marder 38T with its ammo racks ll loaded and odd bits and pieces chucked into the fighting compartment. The vehicle to its left looks to be a 'schwerer Geländegängiger Lasktraftwagen 4·5t für Flak (Sf)' minus its weapon and wheels, but with a handrail to aid mounting and dismounting the gun platform.

NARA

GI's unload a leichte Ladungsträger (Sd.Kfz.302) from the rear of a British signals truck. This model of the 'Goliath' was powered by two electric motors and carried a 60kg explosive charge. **Opposite:** The rear of the vehicle where the telephone guide wire spooled out is painted in a lighter colour to aid the operator in tracking it. Production would switch to a gasoline powered version in early 1944. These diminutive vehicles were issued to the Pioniere and, apparently, some coastal defence strongpoints ('Widerstandsnester'), as few were captured on the landing beaches, making them the only German 'tanks' that actually tried to throw the allies back into the sea. **2x NAF**

The photos on pages 70 through 75 were taken by Cpl. Albin P. Zoremba, Co.A, 116th Regt., 1st Bn, 29th Infantry Division. According to notes accompanying the photos, "*Shortly after the invasion he was attached to the 9th US Army Photo Interpretation Detachment.*" The 116th came ashore on D-Day and suffered heavy losses. It was then committed on Martinville Ridge during the push to Saint-Lô in mid June. Here he stopped to snap a pho of two shovel-wielding GI's standing in front of the burned out Panther Ausf.A from Pz.Rgt.6 that we showed on page 96 of *Panzerwrecks 8*.

D.Potochniak via G.Bradfo

nother Panther and another photo opportunity as an M31 ARV comes up the road. This anther was shown in greater detail on pages 94 and 95 of *Panzerwrecks 8* where it can e seen from the other side. We are indebted to GI's such as Cpl. Zoremba who stopped their jeeps or stepped a few paces out into the hot sun to compose and shoot a photo for posterity. We are further indebted to those who preserved and passed along those same photos so that a wider audience might enjoy them. **D.Potochniak via G.Bradford**

Two images of a Panther Ausf.A from I./Pz.Rgt.6 named 'Chrystel' (whose name was written on the gun travel lock) knocked out by a US M10 tank destroyer outside of La Fauvellerie, the north of Le Dézert. The photo on this page appears to show the vehicle next to a crater, but in fact the photographer has moved behind an earthen bank to fit the tank into the frame. The remains of a bracket for a stowage box can be seen over the engine deck. Further information about this engagement can be found in Didier Lodieu's book *Dying for Saint-Lô - Hedgerow Hell, July 1944.*

2 x D.Potochniak via G.Bradford

We are told that this burned out Panther Ausf.A is from the Stabskompanie of I./Pz.Rgt.6, and carried the tactical number '300.' The bolt-counters among you will have noticed that it has a mix of 16 and 32 bolt road wheels. Its gun was locked in the gun travel lock whe the bottom of the pannier blew out.

D.Potochniak G.Bradfo

The Panther from the previous page is in the background. In the foreground is a schwerer Panzerspähwagen (5cm) (Sd.Kfz.234/2) from Pz.Aufkl-Lehr-Abt.130 that drove into a firestorm of shot and shell. The two were destroyed between Canisy and Le Mesnil-Amey (Saint-Lô/Cobra sector) on 26 July. The coaxial turret MG 42 on the 'Puma' has a flash hider attached to its muzzle. No markings could be detected on the vehicle, even under high magnification.

D.Potochniak via G.Bradford

his schwerer Panzerspähwagen (5cm) (Sd.Kfz.234/2) was destroyed outside Caumont wn hall on 12 June. The resulting explosion blew apart the front hull, separating the mour plates at the weld seams, and fire reduced the tyres down to the steel reinforcing nds. The vehicle appears have been left in its base coat of RAL 7028 'Dunkelgelb', as no camouflage scheme is evident. Note the steel bars welded to the hatches, next to the padlock loop, purpose unknown, and the smoke grenade in the lower smoke discharger on the turret side. Other rods or bars can been seen: horizontally on the rear of the turret roof casting a shadow, sprouting vertically from the roof, by the rear visor, etc. **2x TTM**

The rear of the vehicle seen on the previous pages. An Allied anti-tank shell has holed the 10mm thick rear plate, cracking it in the process. The rear engine access hatch is partially open and shows the white background of a licence plate, but the number is indecipherable. Other photographs show the wreck was subsequently moved next to the building in the background.

Ø.Leonse

These three photos were found in a Canadian technical intelligence report which gave no date or location. The vehicle is surrounded by a low brick wall on two sides, and a building on a third. The Canadians remarked upon the *Commander's hatch showing closely packed ball race for periscope housing"* and the *"Internal views of telescope and gun travelling lock"* seen in the photos above.

3x LAC

Behind this demolished '88' sits a scorched and cracked 'Puma' with a large, outlined tactical number, '152.' The gunner's hatch is open and the periscope for the commander's hatch can been seen above the roof line. The 8·8cm Flak 36 rode on the Sd.Ah.202 trailer with its breech facing the direction of travel and the barrel over the dual rear tyres. T[...] 8·8cm Flak 18 on the Sd.Ah.201 was exactly the opposite, with the barrel pointing in t[...] direction of travel.

VI[...]

...le is left of the turret rear on this 'Puma' from SS-Aufkl.Abt.1. The building in the ...kground can be seen through cracks in the front of the turret as well. The gunner's ...d hatch was hinged to the outside of the roof, allowing it to hang on. Internally, the breech of the 5cm Kw.K. 39/1 effectively separated the gunner from the commander. This photograph was taken in Epaney by Milan Friedler, who fought with the 1st Czechoslovak Armoured Brigade. He photographed this wreck in September of 1944 **M.Friedler**

A walk-around of a burned out 'Puma' taken by US Technical Intelligence personnel who recorded the markings on the breech block and the following [estimated] details concerning the armour: Turret, Front: 30mm at 20°; Sides and rear: 10mm at 20°; Roof: 10mm; Gun mantlet estimated to be 100mm (rounded); Superstructure, Front: 30mm at 30°; Sides: 8-10mm at 25°. Hull, Upper nose: 25mm at 50°; Lower nose: 25mm at 3 Sides: 8mm at 30°; Glacis plate: 15mm at 70°. Less important details include the gr handle and three small fittings on the glacis plate access hatch, and the wire strung up a down and across the turret. A very faint 'W' can be seen painted on the nose. **4x NA**

The bumper is missing, and it looks as though the vehicle was dragged to its current ~~l~~cation. These vehicles were powered by air cooled Tatra V12 diesel engines. **2.** The ~~fra~~me of the engine deck has been twisted off to the right side of the vehicle. **3.** Looking ~~fro~~m the turret towards the rear of the vehicle. Missing are the circular air filters in the bottom left and right corners of the engine compartment that connected to the intake pipes on either side. **4.** Two fans at the rear of the engine sucked air in through the louvres on the engine deck directly behind the turret. The spare tyre, fan belts and all the other rubber components have burned away.

4x NARA

Civilians pose on a schwerer Panzerspähwagen (5cm) (Sd.Kfz.234/2) destroyed on the road from Pacy-sur-Eure to Vernon on 22 August. The vehicle belonged to either SS-Pz.Aufkl. Abt.1 or Pz.Aufkl.Abt.2. The hull escape hatch, between the second and third wheels, hangs down in the open position. This vehicle has the square box on the left side of t engine compartment for the antenna mount for the FU-12 80 watt transmitter.

F.Depr

other casualty at Pacy-sur-Eure, this one on the banks of the river. This is a ...nzerspähwagen P 204 (f) of 3 or 4./Res.Bat. 4.SS.Polizei-Div or Sicherung Regiment 1, once armed with two 7·5mm MGs, rather than the more common 25mm cannon and 7·5mm MG. Note that the French number '20006' has been left intact.

F.Deprun

From a Canadian Technical Intelligence Report:

"Just east of Les Champeaux, a half tracked SP gun was found in a lane. This veh mounted a 20mm gun. The hull was lightly arm'd but there was no turret, the only crew protection being the gun shield. Front view showing gun & rail to prevent the gun from fouling the hull."

The basis for this vehicle was a French Unic Kegresse P 107 half-track with a superstructure believed to be made from the equivalent of quarter inch armour plate. The top right hand corner of the nonstandard gun shield could be removed if necessary. In German service, this armoured version, without the 2cm Flak, was known as the leichter Schützenpanzerwagen U304(f). From the construction details (hinged armour windshields and visors, full width angled armour on the nose and around the gun platform (which allowed full rotation of the gun?), doors, etc, it is evident that this was a well thought out and executed design.

2x LAC

A look at the side of the vehicle shows a fair camouflage pattern underneath the foliage. Th drive sprocket, idler and road wheels were a steel, as we can see from their shiny edges. Th louvred panels on the ground were fitted eithe side of the engine.

LA

mangled Selbstfahrlafette (Sd.Kfz.10/5) für 2cm Flak 38 with 'Behelfspanzerung' with its ⌐un mount at the 8 o'clock position. This vehicle was one of the longest serving designs ⌐ the war and also one of the most photographed vehicles. A six man crew served the ⌐eapon, with two Kanonier charged with passing ammunition from the towed trailer to the loaders on the gun platform. For the crew's protection when dismounted, six rifles were carried, three on each side, in covered fender racks. Wire mesh has been put across the armoured 'windshield' giving the appearance of 'Zimmerit'. Note the Pz.Kpfw.IV lurking in the background.

Ø.Leonsen

A penetrating round through the driver's door on the armoured cab of this 3·7cm Flak 37 auf Selbstfahrlafette (Sd.Kfz.7/2) put an end to its days as a fighting vehicle. Here we can plainly see the normal ground mount for the gun spanning the sagging rear platform. The loaders needed to be mindful of the outriggers when the gunner tracked an aircra crossing side to side. The gun barrel is at the 2 o'clock position and appears to be at i maximum depression of -10°. Additional ammunition would be towed in a trailer. **AM**

Another 3·7cm Flak 37 auf Selbstfahrlafette (Sd.Kfz.7/2), apparently in rather good condition, about to be pushed off the road by a Sherman dozer. A good shove under the gun platform would certainly pop the fold down panels surrounding the platform and allow the ammo to spill out. This view gives us a rare opportunity to see the hatches in the roof of the armoured cab which would allow better observation of low flying aircraft. Note the different size sliding visors in the front plate. With a gun having a high cyclic rate of fire (80 - 100rpm), you would expect to see spare gun barrels carried somewhere, but we have yet to see them carried on these vehicles.

TTM

"US soldiers look over the wreckage to a German vehicle which was towing an 88mm gun when struck during the aerial bombardment of 3000 Allied planes preceding the opening of a new US offensive west of Saint-Lô, July 25 1944." Actually this a Škoda Radschlepper Type 175L towing a 7·5cm Pak 40. The Škoda tractor has had its cab blown off in this instance but the huge, cleated, iron wheels are unmistakable. According to Didier Lodieu's *Dying f[...] Saint-Lô - Hedgerow Hell, July 1944*, Panzer-Lehr-Pionier-Bataillon 130 used these vehicle[...] One was destroyed at Le Dézert, 11 July, near La-Sellerie, and three were captured aroun[...] Marigny during 'Cobra.'

NAR[...]

nother Škoda Radschlepper Type 175L. The front and rear wheels were both 1500mm (4 ot, 10 inch) diameter, but the front wheels were 300mm wide while the rear wheels were 00mm wide. Power was supplied by either a diesel or gasoline engine via two propeller afts. Each shaft drove the wheels on one side of the vehicle only. Maximum speed was 16km/hr. For additional traction on ice, spikes approximately two inches long could be fitted to the wheels. These spikes were carried in compartments between the wheels. This unusual vehicle was also fitted with a winch and mini-spade, shown here held up by a hook and chain. It could tow a 5t load. Note the driver's door is missing.   **L.Archer**

A load carrier version of the 15cm Panzerwerfer 42 typically found in Normandy. The front wheels have been removed, and the rear road wheels are unusual in having holes smaller in diameter than normally seen. The rudimentary caption with the photo states that it wa photographed in the Falaise area.

USAHE

A Canadian officer named Major A.G. Sangster filed a report on enemy AFVs encountered in Normandy. These are his observations on a Panther Ausf.G found in Heurtevent, South of Livarot, probably from II./Pz.Rgt.33 of 9.Panzer-Division. (The vertical anti-spall grid cut into the surface of the 'Zimmerit' to prevent large sections from coming off after small arms fire and shell strikes has been diagonally applied to the turret and gun mantlet, a feature of Panthers assembled by M.A.N.)

. "Panther tk abandoned by roadside near Heurtevent 4571 after bogging and breaking final drive input shaft."

. "Panther co-driver's hatch showing type of spring loading used. This veh was new having registered only 864km."

. "Air cleaner parts as found. This is typical of the way these vehs are found with parts unnecessarily opened up."

. "Interior of Panther fighting compartment showing comds cupola, azimuth control shaft and gun counter-balance spring gear."

. "Azimuth indicator fitted to Panther tk."

5x LAC

1

A Panther Ausf.A, tactical number '234' from 2./Pz.Rgt.3, garnered the attention of at least two photographers: one British, one Canadian, although the le.S.P.W. (Sd.Kfz.250) with an unusual trellis type of antenna may be the most intriguing vehicle in view. The Panther had been disabled near the church in Saint-Lambert sur Dives. **Opposite:** Like so much farm machinery left to rust, AFVs and softskins lie scattered in the dump at Saint-Lambert su Dives. Panther '234' is centre-stage. See which types you can identify.

2x L.Archer/W.Auerbach, 1x D.Trowbridg